VISIBLE THOUGHTS

Shatora R. Gaskin

WORDS MATTER
P U B L I S H I N G
OUR WORDS CHANGE THE WORLD

Words Matter Publishing
P.O. Box 1190
Decatur, IL 62525
www.wordsmatterpublishing.com

ISBN 13: 978-1-962467-67-4

Library of Congress Catalog Card Number: 2025932257

I dedicate this book to
my beautiful daughters, Mommy loves you!

Table of Contents

Little Black Girl

Little Black Girl with the BIG Ol' eyes
and crooked teeth.
Little Black Girl with the kinky hair and
slang in her speech.
Little Black Girl with the bags under her eyes
and the mole on her lip.
The one with the ashy hands and stretched out hips.
Little Black Girl,
I don't know her name
Little Black Girl,
I don't know her pain
Little Black Girl,
Do you know your worth?
Yes, you were made from dirt
But, don't come from dirt
Yes, you were made to be loved by a man
But not controlled by a man
The "Hard-worker" gene is in your DNA
But you were not born to be a slave or enslaved

Little Black Girl,
Do you know your name?
Little Black Girl
How dare you be ashamed?
The elders of your tree were KINGS & QUEENS,
KIND & WISE,
TEACHERS & PHILOSOPHERS,
ROYALS & RULERS,
BLACK & BEAUTIFUL,
Little Black Girl
Why do you look so surprised?
Little Black Girl
You're not defined by what's between your thighs,
Nor the size of your behind,
Nor the shade of your eyes Or the shade
on top of your eyes
Little Black Girl
What is your name?
Little Black Girl
Who didn't cause you pain?
Little Black Girl
There's always music in the rain
Little Black Girl
You are not defined by your pain

Nor your mistakes
Nor your losses
Little Black Girl
No need to live cautious
Take risks,
Live free
Little Black Girl
You are MORE than what society
categorizes you to be.
Little Black Girl
You have the vision of three eyes,
so why can't you see
You are blessed with gifts for the world
There's a message in your speech
Little Black Girl
Is that all you see?

BLACK (Inspired by Black History Month)

I truly love & embrace the skin I'm in.
Black is Beautiful
Black is Bold
Black is Powerful
Black is Strong
Black is Tough
Black Is Wisdom
Black is Empowerment
Black is Motivation
Black is Pure
Black is Nature
Black is often Misunderstood

WEAK

See you think I'm weak because
I don't let your opinions phase me
See you think I'm weak because
I don't let your words intimidate me.
See you think I'm weak because I hardly speak
See you think I'm weak because I think before I speak
See you think I'm weak because
I barely look you in the eyes
See you think I'm weak because
I see you with my third eye
See you think I'm weak because
my emotions rarely show
See you think I'm weak because
I'd rather sing a song than entertain drama
See you think I'm weak because you don't understand
See you think I'm weak because I know who I am

THANK YOU MAMA!

Thank you, Mama,
For all the warm hugs & sweet kisses
Thank you, Mama,
For all the long talks & lessons
Thank you, Mama,
For all the meals you made to fill my stomach
Thank you, Mama,
For rubbing my back when I'm down
Thank you, Mama,
For your tough love & discipline
Thank You, Mama,
For believing in me
Thank you, Mama,
For being my eyes when I couldn't see
Thank You, Mama,
For not being my friend, But my Mother
Thank you, Mama,
For your strong advice

Thank You, Mama,
For always making sure I had the things I need
Thank You, Mama,
For being you
Thank you, Mama,
For your unconditional love
Thank you
Thank you
Thank you, Mama,
I can't say it enough
I Love you!

I AM

I Am Smart
I Am Young
I Am Beautiful
I Am a Healer
I Am a Protector
I Am a Mother
I Am a Daughter
I Am a Niece
I Am a Cousin
I Am a Dear Friend
I Am Patient
I Am Kind
I Am Love
I Am Success
I Am Wealthy
I Am Worthy
I Am Wise
I Am a Helper
I Am Connected
I Am Power
I Am Love
I AM.

IRONIC

See I enjoy being my best company
I don't mind dancing without a mirror
I'd rather wear boxers & Briefs
I like books & pens
Pencils & paper
Soul & music
The moon & the stars
Drums & guitars
See I don't mind a turkey sandwich without mayo
Fries without ketchup
See I like Monkeys & Turtles
Cheetahs & Bears
Lions & Tigers
I like cartoons & comic strips
Cotton candy & funnel cake
Horses & ponies
Cake & Ice cream
Long walks & conversations
I enjoy doing handy work & exercising
I like Jeeps & Rifles

9

Tattoos & Piercings
Space & my thoughts
I really enjoy being my best company

PAIN

PAIN,
It's Ironic because it has four letters just like love, but
doesn't give the same feeling as the emotion love
They say love causes pain, but did you know that you
can learn from pain?
Did you know that you can grow from pain?
Pain caused me to love myself unconditionally
Pain taught me to be strong
Pain helped me grow mentally
Pain taught me not to expect
Pain helped me move on
Pain showed me people's true colors
Pain revealed secrets
Pain caused me to cry
Pain made me smile
Pain made me laugh

TEARS OF A LION

Fearless, Ambitious & gifted
Yet water falls from my eyes at times
Courageous & kind
Yet water falls from my eyes at times
Patient & faithful
Optimistic & poignant
Still water falls from my eyes at times
Why do I cry?
At times I can't pinpoint it
My tears, these tears often fall unexpected
My emotions, these emotions are often neglected
My past taught many lessons
My present is revealing hidden messages
My future is being manifested
Why do I cry?
It's hard to explain
These aren't open wounds
How do I describe Internal pain?
How can you wash away rain?
My tears, these tears

Often fall unexpected
My emotions, these emotions are often neglected
My heart, my soul is forever protected
But still at times water falls from my eyes
No noise at all
Just silent cries
Kindhearted & wise
Yet water falls from my eyes

SPOKEN

These words are spoken no joking, no choking
My mind is open, focused, no loping
These fears are broken, diminished, frozen
These scars are closing, healing, not reopening
These words are spoken
Her mind is floating
Her heart is open
Her voice is coaching
Her dream is approaching
Her worries are departing
Her mission is starting
Failure is starving
Pain is Her struggle
Her struggle is Her story
Her pain is Her glory
Her downfall is her praise
Her lost is her gain
Her journey is the way
These words are spoken
I once was broken

I once was coping
I once was hoping
LOST!
Mind was stumbled
Life was jumbled
Heart was fumbled
Now I stand BOLD
Humbled
Stern
Fearless
Content
Focused
Chosen
These words are spoken

BRICKS & STONES

Growing up I was taught sticks & stones may break
my bones, but words will never hurt me
Then I grew up and realized out of rage words feel
like bricks & stones and do hurt me
Words can feel like rocks & boulders
When intense emotions have no control
words can cut like a knife
Make you feel extremely low
Words can make you second guess your appearance
Words can make you love yourself less
Words can manipulate your mind
Words can make you cry
Growing up I was taught sticks & stones may break
my bones, but words will never hurt me
Then I grew up & realized out of rage words feel like
bricks & stones and do hurt me

FOR THE LOVE OF A MAN

For the love of a man made me lose love for myself.
For the love of a man made me tamper
with my health.
For the love of a man made me go blind.
For the love of a man made me forget who I am.
For the love of a man.
All for the love of a man,
I didn't understand.
For the love of a man, I accepted to be used.
For the love of a man.
All for the love of man,
I didn't understand.
I didn't understand my worth.
He didn't understand my hurt.
I didn't understand my life.
He didn't understand my love.
I didn't understand my control.
He didn't understand my soul.

For the love of a man,
I stumped my growth,
I lowered my worth,
I cried at night,
I sacrificed,
I had to fight,
I had to beg,
I lost my happiness,
I lost my faith
For the love of a man,
All for the love of a man,
I didn't understand.

WHITE ELEPHANTS

Don't think too hard
Just let your mind flow
Don't be hard on yourself
Give time for yourself to grow
Give space for your mind to know
Give love for yourself to glow
Give hope for your soul to sow
Peace is within
Strength is within
Courage is within
Wisdom is within
Endurance is within
Faith is within
Ambition is within
Potential is within
Creativity is within
Your future is within
Your purpose is within

Your calling is within
So don't think too hard
Just let your mind flow
Don't be hard on yourself
Give time for yourself to grow

Brown Butter

Your presence is satisfying
Your personality is overwhelming
Your words are everlasting
Your touches are tender
Your actions are sweet
Brown Butter
Brown Butter
You're so great to me
So patient
So kind with me
Brown Butter
Brown Butter
You're not what I expected but everything I've been
missing and needing
My feelings are bleeding
Emotions are flowing
Constantly thinking about you without you knowing
Brown Butter
Brown Butter

You're more than what I expected
You're more than what I knew
Chocolate Brown
Sweet & Smooth
Rich & Fulfilling
You're my Brown Butter

Surreal

They say looks can be deceiving

So can emotions

See I thought I was falling for you until you truly
perceived your personality

See I thought you were the one until you started
acting like I need you

Emotions can be so deceiving

Finally Free

I sing without a reason
I Smile through every season
I can do my hair anyway I please
I can buy myself the things I need and
the things I want
I can laugh & dance with my family
I can write peacefully
I can spend time with myself
I can love myself
I'm finally free!

I FELL IN LOVE WITH A GIRL

I fell in love with a girl who listens when I think
I fell in love with a girl who fulfills my every needs
I fell in love with a girl who believes in my dreams
I fell in love with a girl who puts me first
I fell in love with a girl who knows my worth
I fell in love with a girl who cares how I look
I fell in love with a girl who listens when I speak
I fell in love with a girl who caresses my scars
I fell in love with a girl who forgives my every mistake
I fell in love with a girl who accepts my every flaw
I fell in love with a girl who wipes every tear
I fell in love with a girl who doesn't care what I wear
I fell in love with a girl who will never leave my side
I fell in love with a girl who loves me unconditionally
I fell in love with a girl
Ironically her name is ME!

CURIOUS SOUL

If the moon could speak
What would it say?
If the stars could sing
What melody would they play?
If trees could hug
Would a tree hug me?
Would a leaf kiss me?
Would the grass caress me?
Would the wind grasp me?
Would the concrete balance me?
Would the rocks befriend me?
Would the Sun look at me?
Would the Air comfort me?
If Earth could speak
Would Earth Acknowledge me?

TWICE MY AGE

The connection was so pure
The intentions felt genuine
I opened up to you fearlessly because your mind
sparked my soul
When you held me, I felt secured
When you talked to me, I felt loved
When you listened, I felt understood
It's something you bring that makes my soul sing
It's something you bring that makes my heart smile
Can I be falling for you?
Despite your age, can you be falling for me even
though you're nearly twice my age?

BLACK SHEEP

Black Sheep
Why do you weep?
Your pupils glazed with tears
How do you see?
Internal destruction
Where's your peace?
You're overlooked, However noticeable
More less powerful
Isolation at its best
Your presence still admirable
Your aura illuminates every space you fill
Your warm heart coats every chill
Loved and envied simultaneously
Projecting your ambition miraculously
Manifesting your imaginations accurately
Black Sheep
Why do you weep?
You are a warrior
You stand out for a reason

You're not understood because you're so different
Your soul is unusual
Black Sheep
You are beautiful
One of a kind
Your rapidly evolving intimidates many
Black Sheep
Your vision is deep
Dreams never sleep
Your trials reap
Black Sheep
Why do you weep?
That doesn't mean you're weak
Black Sheep
Stand tall on your feet

POETIC THOUGHTS

When the stars align, I see a message in the sky
The crystals create shimmers, vibrating
through my mind
What if we could rewind time, rewrite our stories and
start over again?
Would you take that chance?
What if time waited for us?
What if there was no time at all?
These are just poetic thoughts

ILLUSION

Just because the tears aren't visible doesn't
mean they don't fall
Her smile protects the pain
Her confidence hides from doubt
Her potential overrides fear
Her emotions leak discreetly
Just because she laughs doesn't mean she's ok
Just because she finds a solution doesn't mean
she don't complain
Her personality outweighs her attitude
Her actions influence her insight
Just because she's quiet doesn't mean she's timid
Her aura screams out loud
Her eyes reflect quantum visions
Just because the tears aren't visible doesn't mean
they don't fall
Her smile protects her pain
Her confidence hides from doubt
Her potential overrides fear
She's an illusion

SPOKEN Vol. 2

These words are Spoken
My thoughts are floating
My words are potent
My heart is open
Peace is approaching
Lust is departing
Failure still starving
My voice is alarming
These words are spoken
These gifts are tokens
My frequency is coasting
Vibration rising
The Stars, The Moon, and I aligning
Self-doubt, lack of courage, and I dividing
I was once searching
Soul was hurting
Emotions were broken
Now I stand replenished
Knowledge-toting
These words are SPOKEN!

WOLF IN MY FIELD

There's a Wolf in my field who crushes
every flower that blooms
Grass covered in gloom
There's a wolf in my field that barks and grunts
No matter how hard I try to groom and make room
for this wolf, he wanders in my space
Hibernating energy darker than a blackout
No matter how gentle I am, he mimics depressed
emotions, upset emotions, sad emotions
There's a wolf in my field who fills it
with negative emotions
There's a wolf in my field that taunts and haunts
A wolf that steps on generosity
There's a wolf in my field
I just wish he would leave

WORDS FROM THE HEART

I'm going to love you unapologetically
Our souls will conjoin, dancing to
the rhythm of true love
My shoulder will be a bucket catching every tear
My arms will be a safe haven for your worries
You are a masterpiece in my heart that I'm
manifesting vividly
You are an awaiting blessing
I'm going to hug you so tight, you won't even gasp
Tender touches that always last
Unforgettable moments
Genuine laughs
No thoughts of the past
No worries about what we have
Let's make an investment in us, put our love in a stash
I believe everything happens when it's supposed to
I believe I will meet you when I'm supposed to
I'm all for you
I will show you
I will hold you in my heart and mind because I
believe we will meet when we're supposed to

MYSELF/SOLITUDE

We think we know ourselves without
really knowing ourselves
We think we love ourselves before
even finding ourselves
Scared to be alone, but how can you love yourself?
Learn yourself? If you're not by yourself
I thought I needed a significant other to feel whole
I thought I needed a "boyfriend", a "Man" to
complete my soul
I thought I needed "Friends" to make
my memories complete
All I need is my drive, my dedication and
my faith to succeed
Being alone is hard, but learning to love
myself was even harder
Drowning in solitude
Content with the understanding that everything isn't
meant for me to be a part of
I had to study myself, become best
friends with myself

Yes, it gets a little harder
I found myself and moved smarter
It was in that moment I realized it was a part of me
that I found that was missing to fill that spot
I had to love myself

LAYERS OF BEAUTY

I met this guy 24hrs ago and it felt like
I knew him forever
He was so clever
He asked my name
He said I want to call you beautiful but your face is
covered with unnecessary beauty enhancements
I can't even see the real you
Are your eyes really blue?
He said I don't mean to be rude,
but your hair, this you?
He said I want to see how well you wear your face
when it's bare
He was so rare
I felt so weird, but the interest that he showed in me
was mind blowing
I felt so attacked
Then he took my hand and explained it's not that
He said I felt your Aura

Your soul whispered and I heard it
He said you're beautiful and I know it
Behind those layers of beauty you're just an illusion
and I know it

Missing Memories

My heart wanted you to stay
Perhaps you weren't the one for me
I wrote your name in the palm of my hand 47 times
Isn't that insane?
I drew a comic strip from the memories of us but the
characters didn't come out the same
I figured I can manifest you back into my life even if
things aren't the same
I loved you harder than my fist
Still you left me hurting
My heart wanted you to stay
Perhaps you weren't the one for me
I made a quilt out of all the clothes you left behind
I even stitched "I Love You" on the line
I don't know what's going through my mind
Perhaps I miss you
That's why I can't let you go
My heart wanted you to stay

I CHOOSE ME

I choose me after choosing you failed
Love didn't prevail, but evil excelled
Biting into a rotten apple that doesn't hold a smell
Hope never sailed
I kept hitting the same wall, but didn't realize
until I fell
I choose ME!
After crying into my own arms, after caressing and
healing my own scars
I choose ME Now!
When I should've chosen me first, should've loved
hard on myself first
I chose us first
I put lust first
Now look who's hurt
I choose me after choosing you failed
Love didn't prevail
Disappointment I inhaled
Regret I exhaled
I choose ME!

SISTER CODE

Mom always told me them girls not your friends
What is a friend?
My definition of a friend is a person who ride it out
with you, good or bad, thick and thin
A person that's honest with you no matter
how bad it hurts
Never steal from you or turn their back on you
Your home girl for real, not pretend
What ever happened to the sis code?
If we came together, we leave together
What ever happened to sisterhood?
Females sticking together
Uplifting one another to see each other win
Casual outings and gatherings because
the energy is genuine
What ever happened to loyalty?
Mom always told me them girls not your friends

UNCERTAINTY

Warm, sweet sensation
Heart-melting
Soul sparking
Long meaningful conversations
I know you
I'm familiar with you
Everytime you come around
I'm unsure of your duration
Unsure if I should fall into admiration
with your presence
Last time you came around our time didn't last long
Did I leech on too fast?
Everytime the energy of you flows into my heart
My world becomes a standstill unconditionally
Even when I'm unsure of you, I understand still
Love you fill me up and tear me down
Repetitively misleading my emotions until my tears
fall down just as well as my smile
Finally realizing Love,
You love me just as much as I love you

THANK YOU WITH GRATITUDE

I Distanced myself from love
I told myself I was done falling in love
I planned on spending forever alone
I planned on letting no one in my heart home
I planned on growing old alone
I planned on creating memories alone
I planned on developing experiences on my own
I planned and prepared to be myself long term
Then you came along
You came into my life effortlessly
The way you treat me changed my
attitude towards love
The way your hand locks with mine,
I can tell I'm secured
Your kisses are everlasting
Your hugs are filled with passion
Your sweet words warms my soul

I distanced myself from love and told myself I was
done falling in love until you came and changed my
attitude on love
I had a change of heart
A change of mind
Thank you with Gratitude

MAGIC IN YOUR EYES

When I look at you
I see a reflection of the stars
Looking into your soul it's like a reflection of Mars
So much space and gravity for me to fill your heart
When I look into your eyes
I see a spark
A spark that glistens
Your smile is my mission
I want to love you forever
I just need your permission
I see magic in your eyes and I can tell
it's not a disguise
I see magic in your eyes
Your silence is so wise
I see abundance in our lives
Your smile is so nice
Can we kiss under the moonlight?
I see magic in your eyes and it feels more than right

SHE DANCES WITH BLADES

Emotions at its best
Nowhere to release
No one to listen
She dances with her pain
As the blade glistens
A silent cut through her flesh
Her pain listens
Tears and blood simultaneously dripping
What is life? If no one cares for her existence
A second cut through her flesh
The blades are persistent
She partners with the blades
Her pain is persistent
The blades plus her rage causes collision with
a pattern of silent cuts
She's just wishing that her pain will die away

THE POWER OF PEACE

The grass whispers in elegance
My mind manifests your presence
No trace of the tears but the smiles are evident
Calm and anxious
Still faithful and patient
A cycle of hard times
It's time to break the matrix
It's time to break bad habits
I haven't mastered growth yet but I'm good at it
Put your hands in mine
Let our eyes marry one another
Trauma has the best of me
I apologize if my feelings are undercover
Cherish a man who don't want to only
see you under covers
Discouraged by lust
Optimistically waiting for my lover

When will I discover the power of peace?
The power of me
The power of magic
The power of dreams
I cared too much
My feelings are deceased
I tried too hard
Your heart wasn't in my reach
I gave too much
People took advantage of me
I don't speak on too much
THE POWER OF PEACE!

SOUND OF FALL

The sound of Fall is a nice cool breeze
The sound of Fall is leaves falling from the trees,
changing colors from red to yellow
and orange to green
The sound of fall is when you hear kids
making a pile of leaves
diving into them laughing happily

A POEM FOR VICTORIA

Through my years of pain and tears of crying
you've always been by my side
Even though these words couldn't explain
my love for you
I will try to
You're the closest person to my heart
Anytime I'm alone, you bring the light when
I'm in the dark
You're my shoulder when I need comfort
You're my legs when I can't walk
You're my mouth when I can't talk
I couldn't ask for anyone better
I cherish you a lot
No matter how old I get, you treat me the same
When they ask who I admire
I say your name
The warmth of your hugs and the glow of your smile
makes me feel alive again

The bond we have is unexplainable which is funny
because I just explained half
I love you
You always understand me
Sometimes I wish I could call you Mommy

VISIBLE THOUGHTS

Soaked in poetry
Writing words is like therapy
Quiet setting and a calm mind
These thoughts are expressed openly
Writing freely from the mind
Poetry opens me
Sentences flowing so cordially
Emotions expressed clearly
Thoughts are visible vividly
There's nothing like Poetry
I live inside Poetry
Soaked in Poetry
Writing words is like therapy

LITTLE BLACK BOY

Little Black Boy with the beady eyes and nappy braids
Little Black Boy with the fitted caps, fresh
brush and waves
Little Black Boy with the involvement of multiple
women, no sense of commitment due to
how he was raised
Little Black Boy with a huge heart full of pain that's
bound to turn into rage
Little Black Boy
I don't know his name
Little Black Boy
I can sense his pain
Little Black Boy you are not your mistakes
Little Black Boy
Do you know who you are?
Far from a thug
Your ambition exceeds the perception of others
assuming you sell drugs

Little Black Boy
I know it hurts
No male guidance in your life just makes it worse
Little Black Boy you are more than bail bonds
and gang signs
Your elders made change
You reap books, Scholarships, businesses and jobs
Little Black Boy Life doesn't define you
Never forget the greatness you bring
Little Black Boy You are a blessing and A KING!

WICKED SMILES

Baffled by reality,
I accept the confusion
Me wanting you more than you want me
That's unbalance
I decline the toxic infusion
I yearn for direct conclusions
This world is just a dishonest illusion

PEACE ON EARTH is what my soul is Swimming in
The arms of hidden agendas is what I keep falling in
Wicked Smiles
Wicked trials

I read Souls like files
I study and observe energy
There's nothing but evil grins behind
those Wicked Smiles

www.ingramcontent.com/pod-product-compliance
Lightning Source LLC
Chambersburg PA
CBHW030518130626
46549CB00007B/3053